In Control

Dave Boyle
Wendy Pitt

CAMBRIDGE UNIVERSITY PRESS

Published by the Press Syndicate of the University of Cambridge
The Pitt Building, Trumpington Street, Cambridge CB2 1RP
40 West 20th Street, New York, NY 10011–4211, USA
10 Stamford Road, Oakleigh, Victoria 3166, Australia

In association with Staffordshire County Council

© Cambridge University Press 1992

First published 1992

Printed in Great Britain by Scotprint Ltd, Musselburgh

Designed and Produced by Gecko Limited, Bicester, Oxon.

A catalogue record of this book is available from the British Library.

ISBN 0 521 40629 3

PICTURE ACKNOWLEDGEMENTS

Cadbury Ltd. 25b.
Christopher Coggins 4tr, 4cl, 4bl, 5, 6, 7, 8, 9, 10, 11, 12, 13, 14, 15t, 18, 19, 20, 21, 22tr, 22tl, 25tl, 25tr, 26bl, 27, 28, 29, 30
Robert Harding Picture Library 4br, 15bl, 23, 24tr, 26tl, 26br.
Redferns 17.
St. Leonard's Primary School, Stafford 6, 7, 11.
Tescos Supermarket, Bicester 18tr, 18cl, 18br, 19, 20b, 26bl.
Valiant Technology Ltd. 15br.
Zefa Ltd. 22b, 24tl, 24bl, 24br, 26tr.

Picture Research by Linda Proud

NOTICE TO TEACHERS

The contents of this book are in the copyright of Cambridge University Press. Unauthorised copying of any of the pages is not only illegal but also goes against the interests of the authors.

For authorised copying please check that your school has a licence (through the Local Education Authority) from the Copyright Licensing Agency which enables you to copy small parts of the text in limited numbers.

Contents

Home and away   4

Market Forces   18

Home and Away

Talking together

What sort of machines are shown in the pictures?

How are they different?
How are they the same?

How do they make things easier?

Can you think of any other machines like this that are used in homes or in shops?

4

How are these machines controlled?

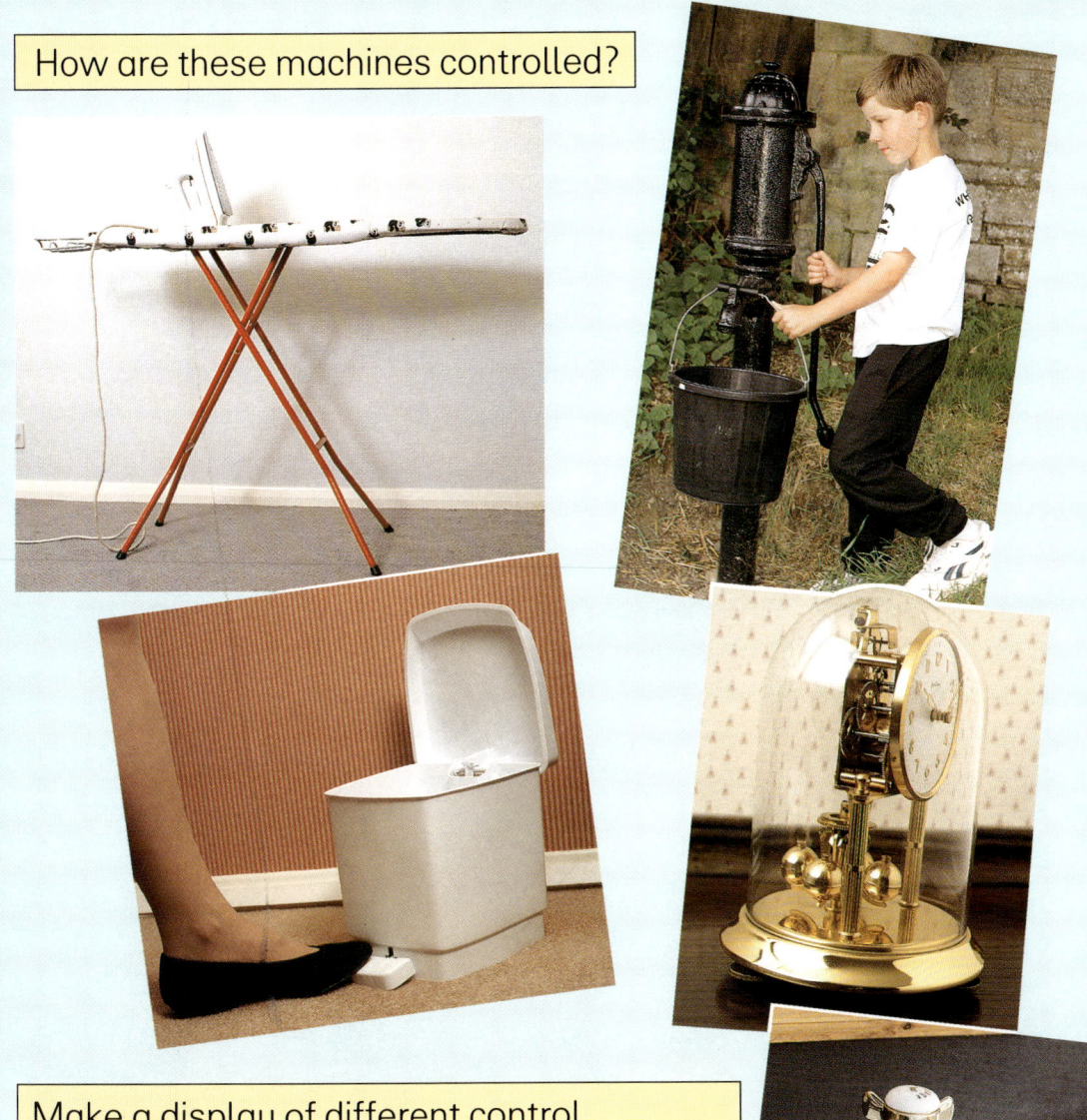

Make a display of different control systems such as, switches, levers, mechanisms, computer.
This could be a mixture of pictures from books and magazines, sketches, photographs, models and real control mechanisms.

Discuss these questions with your teacher and your friends. This will help you to get some ideas.

5

The need

Think of a machine that could make your life easier at home.

Design and make a model of it. It could have several working parts such as a motor, lights, and a buzzer or bell. Make a control unit to operate the machine.

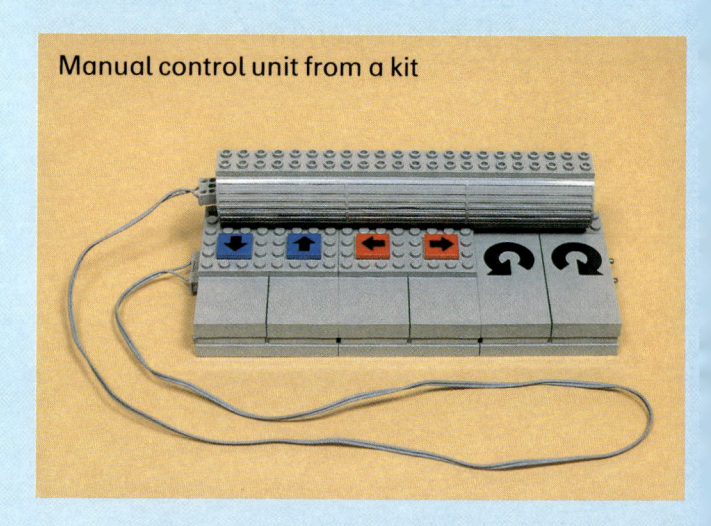

Manual control unit from a kit

•DATA FILE•
Electricity

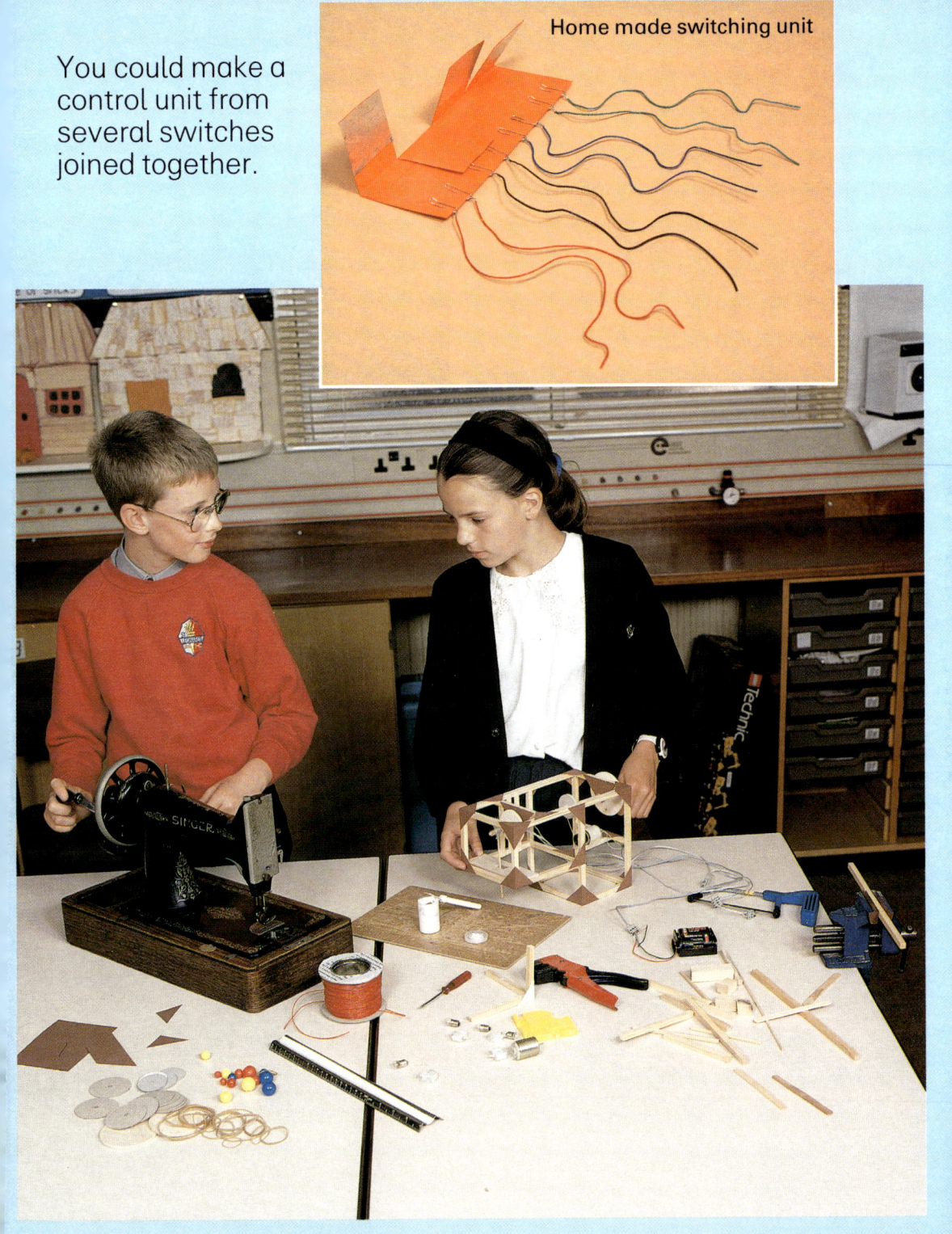

You could make a control unit from several switches joined together.

Home made switching unit

Developing your design

What sort of machines would make your life easier at home?
These pictures may give you some ideas.

Can you see which control systems (gearing, switches, computer) are used to make them work?

· D A T A F I L E ·

Electricity:
switches
Gears and pulleys
Gears
Mechanisms
Pulleys

8

How will you control your model?

What parts of your machine need to be controlled?

Could you control the working parts with simple switches?
What switches would you use?
Would you need a switch to operate your machine forward and in reverse?
Consider using automatic switches. Could you make a switch that stops the machine automatically in the event of danger?

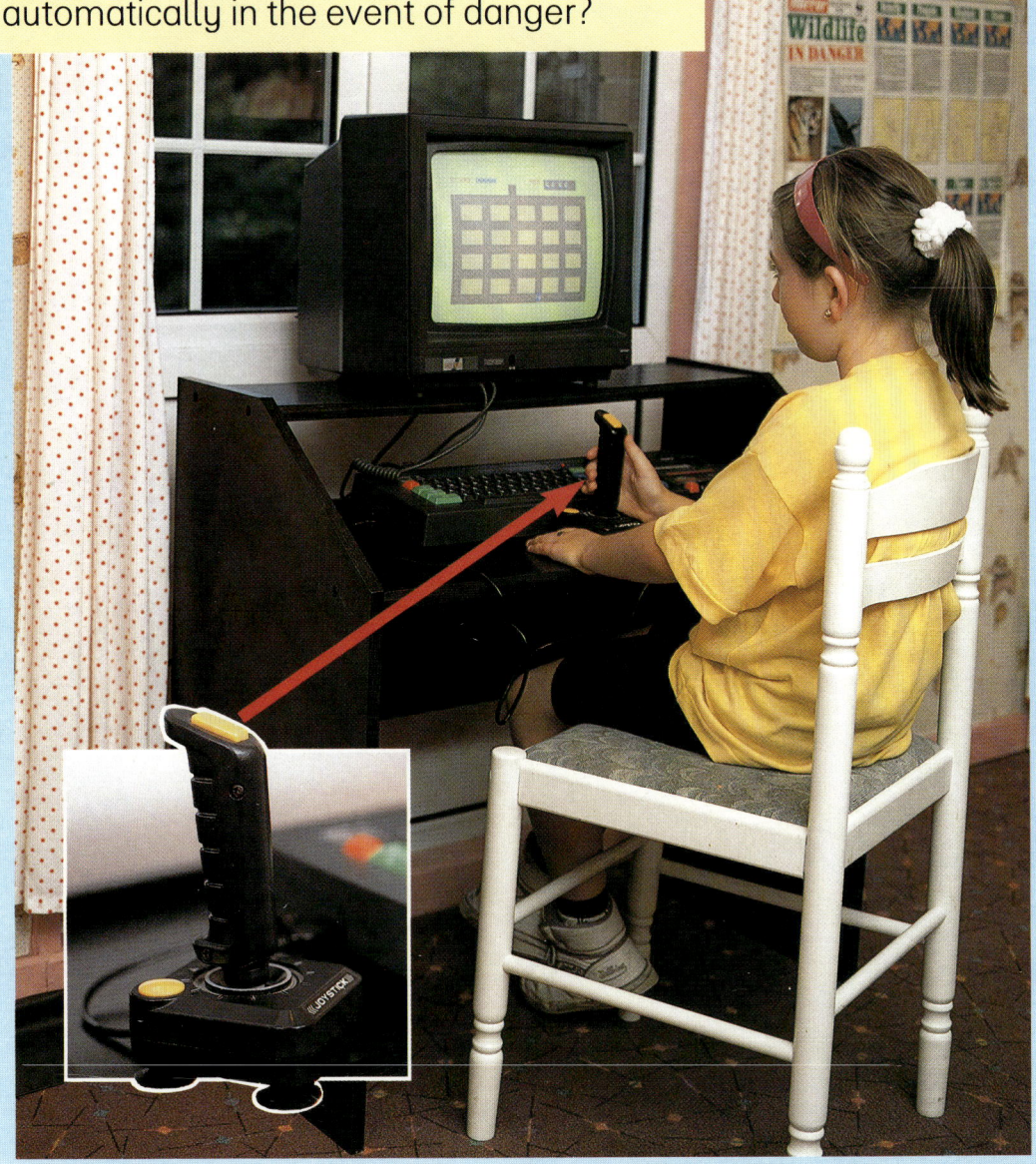

to motor

A home-made reversing switch

to batteries

Try different mechanisms to operate your switches.

> • D A T A   F I L E •
> **Electricity:**
> switches
> **Mechanisms**
> **Hydraulics/pneumatics:**
> using syringes

11

Use gears or pulleys

13

Electronic and computer control

Use a simple electronics kit.

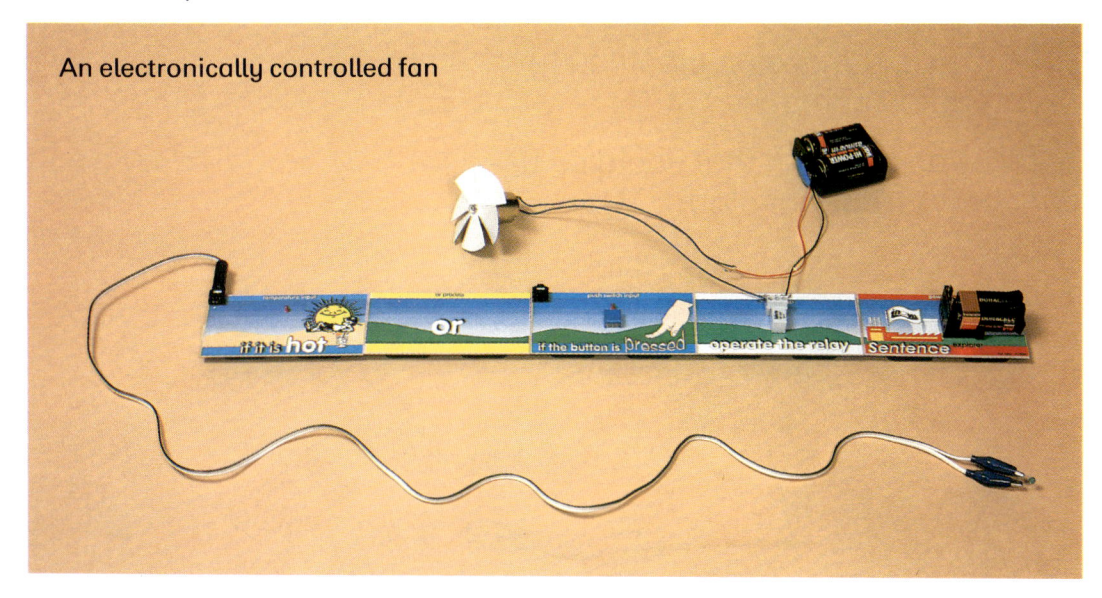

An electronically controlled fan

Use computer control.

• D A T A   F I L E •

**Electricity
Uses of information
technology**

15

More ideas

Design and make an electrically controlled game.

Develop a switch that could be used to operate a burglar alarm.

Design an automatic lighting system for when visitors call at night.

Make a machine that would bring the washing in automatically if it rained.

Devise a system of flashing party lights.

Market Forces

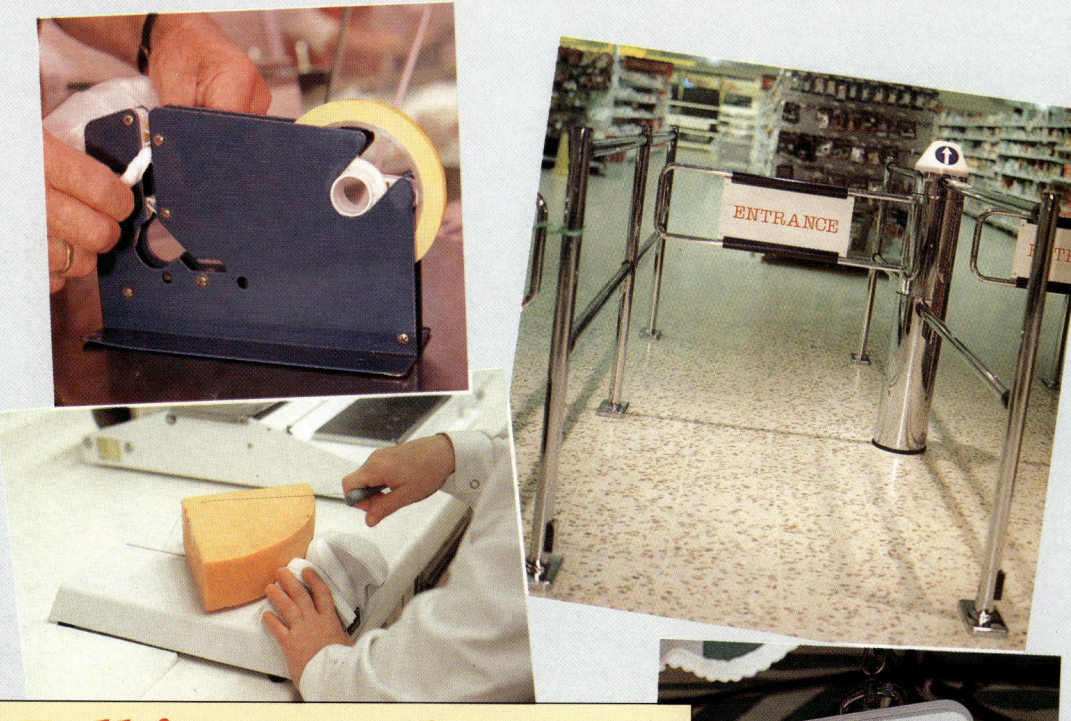

Talking together

What is a machine?

Which machines do we use everyday?
Which machines are used in school?
How do the machines in the picture make life easier?
Which mechanisms are being used?
Why are they used?
How do they work?

Make a list of all the machines used in your local supermarket.

The need

Imagine a local supermarket is having problems moving things around the shop and the warehouse. How could you make life easier for them?

You need to decide what the shop sells and develop a system which will move things around more efficiently.

• DATA FILE •

**Systems
Movement**

Developing your design

What sort of items need moving?
How big are they?
How heavy are they?
Are they fragile?

Where have they to be moved from, and where to?
Do they need to be moved slowly and carefully or can they be moved quickly?
Which different ways could be used to move them?

Consider:
trolleys,   a conveyor belt,
a container system,   an overhead crane,
a fork lift truck,   chutes.
rollers,

Which method would be most suitable?

20

Simple structures

Make a container to carry things or a structure which could be used to help move them.

• D A T A F I L E •

**Structures
Movement**

Levers or linkages

These can be used to move things more easily.

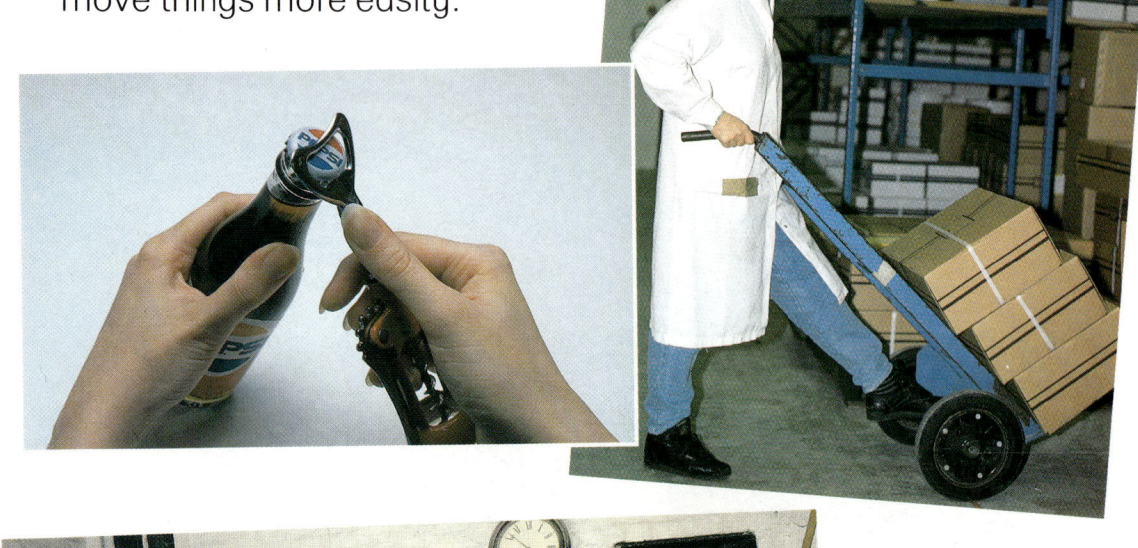

Pulleys and gears

Use pulleys and belts to lift, carry or drag things.

Would chutes be useful?

> • DATA FILE •
> **Gears**
> **Gears and pulleys**
> **Pulleys**

24

You may need to use a system of rollers.

You could try a conveyor belt system.

cotton reels

corrugated card

paper belt/or elastic bands

corrugated card wrapped around cotton reels

A home-made conveyor belt

Kit model of a conveyor belt

Explore simple gearing systems.

Use a construction kit to try various ideas for gearing.

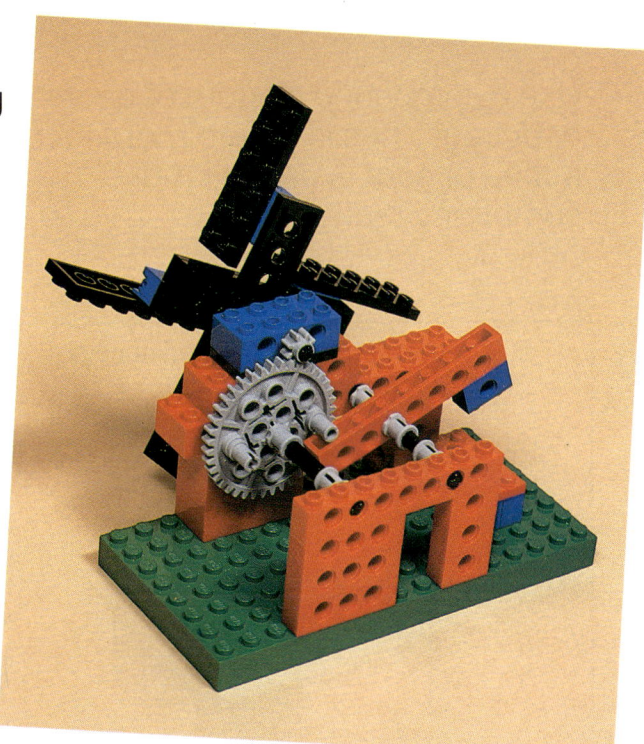

• D A T A   F I L E •
Gears

Use a compound system of gears or pulleys. This is where more than one pulley or gear is used to move something really slowly.

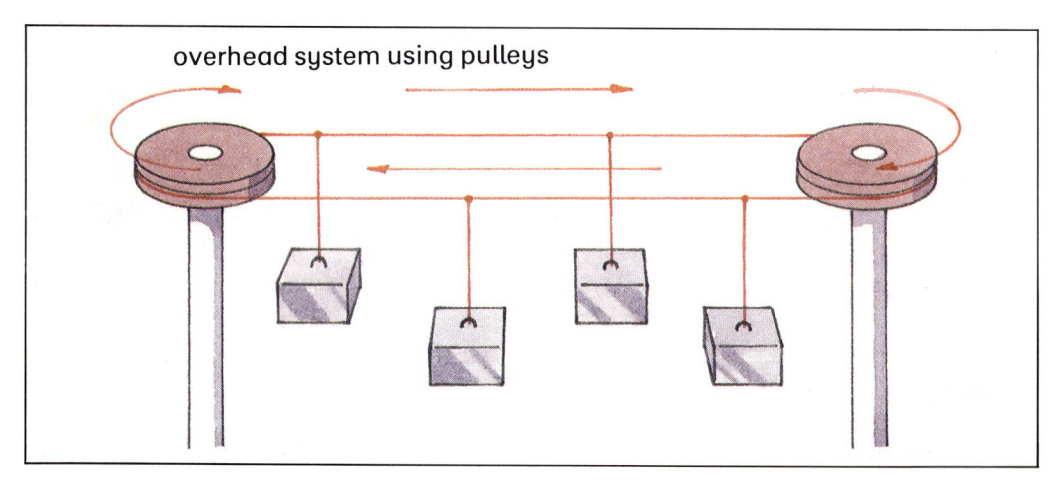

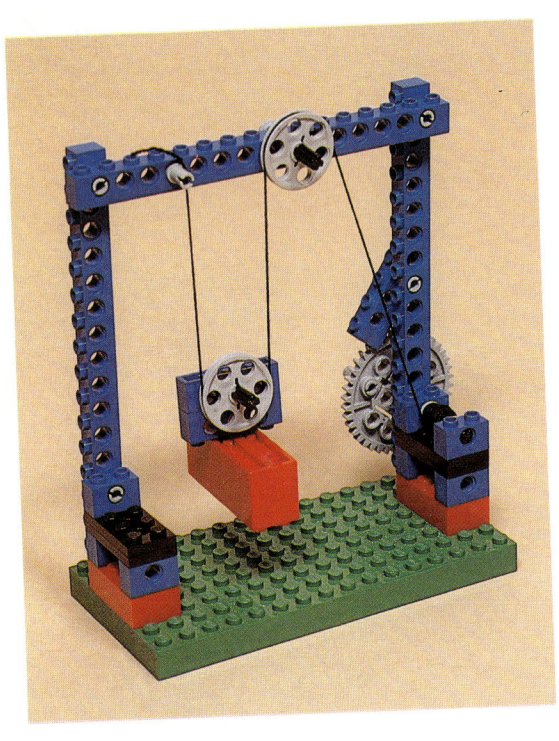

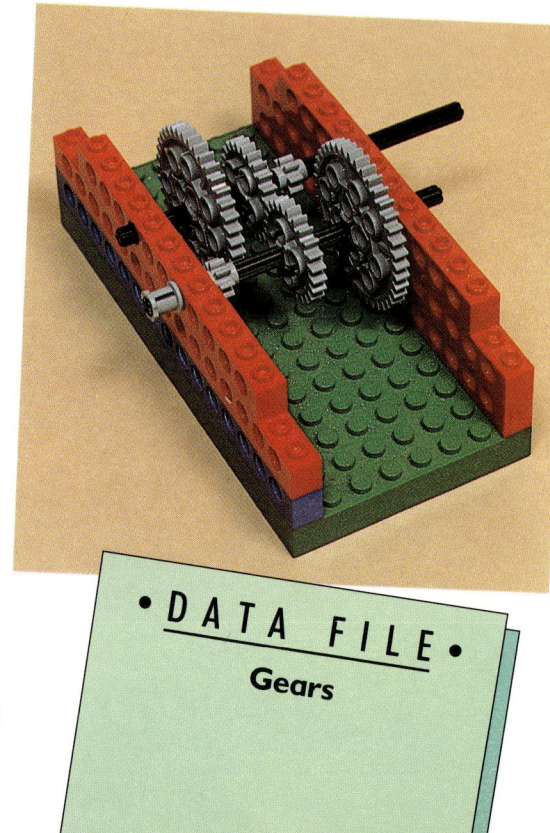

overhead system using pulleys

• DATA FILE •

Gears

Everyday materials can be used to make your own pulleys and gears.

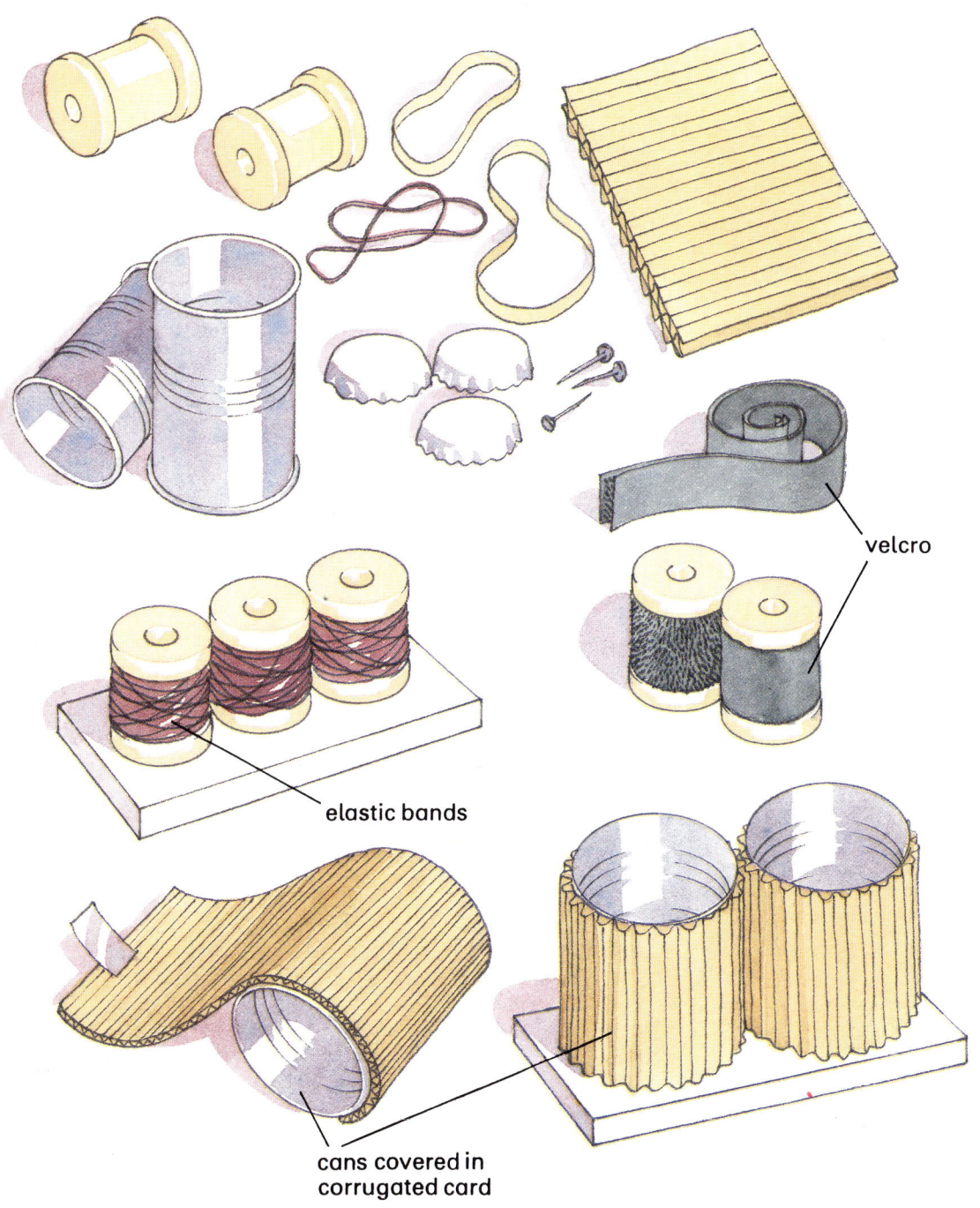

velcro

elastic bands

cans covered in corrugated card

More ideas

Design and make machines which could be used to:

carry something across a gap;

move something really slowly;

position an object accurately;

work a signal;

open doors automatically;

operate a fairground ride.